LEADING GENERATION

EMERGING AS A LEADER IN YOUR GENERATION

5 PRINCIPLES EVERY LEADER UNDER 30 SHOULD DISCOVER

DUERRE AND SHARAI THOMAS

Making A Difference Publishing
23505 Ferndale Avenue
Port Charlotte Florida, 33980
http://mad4u-24.wix.com/madpub

Ordering Information:
Quantity sales. Special discounts are available on quantity purchases by corporations, associations, and others. For details, contact the publisher at the address above.
Orders by U.S. trade bookstores and wholesalers. Please contact Tel: (242) 439-5504; 0r: (941) 234-4461 or visit

http://mad4u-24.wix.com/madpub.

Printed in the United States of America

Cover design: Dreamers Media group

ISBN 13: 978-0-9857798-2-5

ABOUT THE AUTHORS

Pastor Duerre and Sharai Thomas are Leaders in their Generation. Both have been in full time ministry for over 11 years and counting. Duerre has served in many different Leadership capacities, first as a Youth Pastor for 7 years at Calvary Temple Assemblies of God. Under his direction the youth ministry Generation Making A Difference (M.A.D) grew into a world class teen and young adult ministry. Youth Summit, an annual youth conference held by the church grew into one of the largest youth conferences in the Bahamas, while under his direction. Sharai helped to develop an incredible youth worship team for Generation M.A.D serving along with her husband. Both have received international and national recognition for their contribution to youth development; from both Government and Religious organizations. Sharai received recognition as a gospel recording artist, and Pastor Duerre as a coveted youth and young adult speaker.

Thousands of people are impacted every year as a result of their testimony. God had healed Pastor Duerre from a rare blood disorder called lupus. Given up to die, by doctors at the age of 18, he is still alive by Gods grace spreading the word. Sharai grew up as a Pastor's kid but had her shares of life's ups and downs. This dynamic couple founded and now leads one of the fastest growing churchs' on the island of Exuma, Bahamas. They have been Lead Pastors for 4 years and many lives are being changed as a result of their ministry. They are also the C.E.O's and founders of M.A.D Publishing. While there is so much they can be proud of one of their greatest accomplishments, if you were to ask them, would be parenting four incredible sons; D'mari, Damir, Shamir and Dashaun Thomas. History is still being penned for these young leaders.

CONTENTS

DEDICATION

This book is dedicated to our four sons, D'mari, Damir, Shamir and Dashaun Thomas. We pray that through our lives they are influenced to become world class leaders in their generation.

To two of the greatest leaders that influenced our generation, the late Dr. Myles and Ruth Munroe. Their life's theme and mission was to "Rob the grave and die empty." Dr Munroe has inspired us to use our gifts and abilities to impact our generation.

The late Lavard and Radel Parks and their little boy; five year old Jo-Jo this book is in honor of them as well.

We also dedicate this writing to Relevant Kingdom Center, the people who have allowed us to develop and exercise our leadership abilities in their lives every day. We love our Church!

Last but not least to every Emerging Leader, that will read the pages of this book; we dedicate this writing to you. It is our prayer that somehow you are inspired, to become the leaders God intended. You have a purpose and we believe in you!

Endorsements for L.G

President Roland Reagan once said, "Freedom is never more than one generation away from extinction." What he meant by that was the importance of a younger generation arising who is willing to fight for the same freedoms their parents had fought for, to rise to quality leadership that both understands what it takes to lead, but is also willing to live that way and sacrifice for it. In that light, there is a great need for current young leaders who are already making a difference, who understand the necessary disciplines for healthy ministry to speak to their own generation. Pastor Duerre Thomas is one of those young leaders whom God is using to build His church. He has learned some of the key issues in leadership to lead the next generation to do great things for God. It is a blessing that he is willing to share these principles, I hope many will read and benefit from the insights he shares in this book.

Rev. Dennis Marquardt – District Superintendent of Northern New England Assemblies of God, and General Presbyter for the Assemblies of God USA. Dennis Also served as Sr. Pastor of the Assembly of Christian Center in Vergennes, VT. For 24 years; Youth Pastor in the Washington D.C. Area for 3 years, and as a rural pastor in Golden Valley, North Dakota for one year.

I have known Pastor Duerre for many years and since the time I had met him he has always displayed a heart and a passion for God. This is why it is no surprise to me, that this book is a powerful masterpiece that will help emerging leaders understand how to become successful in every facet of life! I can guarantee you that if you read this book from cover to cover it will give you much wisdom and insight that you will find to be priceless.

Dr. Raymond Eneas
Church of Compassion (Lead Pastor)
www.raymondeneas.com

I have grown to love and respect Pastor Duerre Thomas and it is a privilege for me to endorse this book. Duerre is a fine young leader himself, a man of integrity who practices the principles he articulates in this volume. I believe every young, or not so young, leader will benefit from the wisdom he shares in this writing.

Daniel R. Abbatiello, MA, ACC
Dan is an author, leadership development coach and the Director of Church Development for the Northern New England District of the Assemblies of God. His responsibilities include Church Health, Leadership Development and Church Planting. Dan has also served as a lead pastor and denominational leader.

Pastor Duerre Thomas is a knowledgeable, motivating, forward-thinking leader whom God has equipped with spiritual insight and wisdom regarding leadership. He is an encouraging and influential leader that has the ability to cultivate the leadership qualities in those he encounters and mentors.

"Emerging as a Leader" is a guide using biblical truths to propel the young leader to their God ordained potential. Beginning pastoring at the age of twenty-one, I would have welcomed this empowering resource to keep me focused, motivated, and on the right track.

Pastor Nathan Hundley
Lead Pastor Trinity Lighthouse Church
Dayton Ohio: **http://www.tlhchurch.com**

INTRODUCTION

"Trapped within every follower is a hidden leader."

-Dr. Myles Munroe

What is leadership? There are so many definitions of what a leader is that I've come across over the years. But one definition in particular has stuck with me all throughout my life and it is a definition John Maxwell brought to light. It is a one word definition that I believe will stick with you also and that word is: **INFLUENCE.** A leader is simply someone with influence. Some leaders have more influence than others, but the common trait with all leaders no matter what area of life they are in is **INFLUENCE.** All of us are influenced by and are influencing someone around us. Those whom you consider leaders are people that in your opinion have some influence in your life and people who you influence look to you for guidance and direction, that's called leadership.

"The key to successful leadership today is influence, not authority." — Kenneth Blanchard

POSITION DOESN'T NECESSARILY MAKE YOU A LEADER. You can have a title to your name but if no one is following you then you're not much of a leader. The greatest leaders are those that people, not necessarily have to follow but want to follow. These are the ones who genuinely impact people's lives in one way or the other, in a significant way. It is my opinion that in every generation God raises up leaders, these leaders emerge in every sphere of life, from Business, Arts and culture Politics, Education to Religion. There are even areas we overlook as leadership. For example if you are a Mother or Father by default you are a leader. If you have influence in any area and with anyone, you are a leader. The question you must answer is "What kind of leader are you or what kind of leader will you become?"

LEADERS ARE VESSELS. Paul, who was one of Gods greatest leaders in the area of the Church and ministry, and one whose letters make up most of what we call the New Testament, wrote to his young protégé Timothy some very insightful observations. Paul wrote, "In a great house there are *vessels.*" that's why I made the statement earlier "that in every generation God raises up leaders" Paul goes on to say *"There are vessels of gold and silver but also of wood and earthenware, and some for noble use, some for ignoble."* So according to Paul there are two kinds of vessels noble ones and ignoble ones. This is certainly a fact. You have vessels in your house today that you use, preserve and even place in an expensive china cabinet for display, you also have vessels that you use to put trash in, those you only use one time and dispose of that are not all that useful to you. You don't display these ignoble vessels. So the question still looms, "What kind of Vessel (Leader) are you or will you become?" As Paul continues his challenge and encouragement to this emerging leader Timothy he states: *"If anyone purifies himself from what is ignoble, then he will be a vessel for noble use, consecrated and useful to the master of the house, ready for any good work."* 2 Timothy 2:20-21 RSV. God wants to use you for every good work; He wants you to be ready and prepared.

WHY IS LEADERSHIP LIKEND TO A VESSEL? Vessels are used to pour into with the expectation they will pour out. Leaders are committed to being used to make an impact in someone else's life. God doesn't display us in a shelf; rather he displays us on a stage. He wants to show you off. You are called out of darkness or mediocrity on to the stage of life, the lights are shining on you, so you can be an example and an influence to others so that they may see the impact you're making and praise your God who is in heaven. That was the Duerre Thomas' remix to 1 Peter 2:9. God has poured out his spirit on this generation, as a result he expects us to make progress, and have productive lives. He has poured Himself into us, so He can pour out through us.

This is a concept I have come to understand, having the humbling opportunity to be on stages both in the Bahamas and in different parts of the world, through speaking to hundreds and thousands of people, at youth conferences, seminars, schools and business corporations. I understand that I am only a vessel who God uses to point people in His direction, through my gift and abilities. Your stage might be different from mine, but it's still a stage. Someone has their eyes on you, watching your every move, listening to your words and being influenced by your life.

I believe that God wants to use you to be a vessel, a leader of honor and noble use, one whose life will bring praise to Him, regardless of your sphere of influence. This book is meant to give you principles that will help you discover how to become a world class, godly Leader one who will use his or her influence to make a lasting and great impact on this world in a positive way. As a young Leader myself, there are times that these principles have truly helped me to stay the course and understand why God has called me to do what I am doing. When I think about the fact that I am a Vessel, my prayer is often, "God allow my life to make you smile." so that when my assignment is complete I can hear "Well done Good and faithful servant." As you read through the pages of this book I believe you will glean insight that will prepare you for the stage God is ready and waiting to set you on.

DISCOVER YOUR PASSION

1

"If a man has not discovered something that he will die
for, he isn't fit to live.
— Martin Luther King Jr.

Leaders are discovered through a burden. The question most of us
would ask is how? Well first let's get a working definition for that
powerful word "Burden"

"A load that is heavy, something carried, an oppressive or
unpleasant situation that you have to deal with or worry about"

Leaders are born out of adversity. When I think of oppressive
issues such as civil rights Dr. Martin Luther King Jr. emerged as a
leader, as a result of that difficult and heavy load on a race or class
of people. Men like the late Nelson Mandela discovered his
potential behind prison bars and emerged as the President of South
Africa. Leaders in the Reformation period of the church emerged
as a result of the issues that arose within Christianity. Leaders such
as Martin Luther, who wrote the 95 thesis, one of which read "the
Just shall live by faith," as a response to the burden he felt which
religious leaders were taking advantage of parishioners. Johannes
Gutenberg the inventor of the first printing press, along with John
Wycliffe, John Hus and William Tyndale emerged as leaders when
they responded to the need of making sure every person can read
the scriptures for themselves, not just those educated in Greek and

Latin. Men and women with successful political and business careers emerged as powerful leaders because they responded to a crisis or an unpleasant, oppressive issue that was current. We can trace back through time and history that through every crisis, or adverse situation, leaders emerged. One of the leaders we will talk about more in depth further down that emerged from a burden or crisis is Nehemiah.

However, one of the greatest leaders to ever walk the face of the earth, heavens hero, earths emancipator, Jesus, emerged as a result of the greatest crisis man has ever known, the crisis of sin and disobedience. Jesus came into the world and was crucified because of the burden of sin that separated mankind from their Creator and to restore that relationship. However, He did not stay in a grave, but rose as a conqueror and sits at the right hand side of the Father, making intercession for you and me.

PERSONAL CRISIS

While we can look back over national Burdens, very rarely do we recognize that leaders are birthed through personal issues in their lives. As I look at men such as the late Dr. Myles Munroe, one person, to whom I have dedicated this book. When you examine his life and testimony, he emerged as a leader because of personal crisis, which hit his life. One day there was a teacher that told him he was invaluable because of the color of his skin and said some very derogatory remarks about him. As a result his self-esteem was shot down; he went home crying and told his parents what had happened and his mother told him not to go to bed that night until he had read a scripture she had given to him. That scripture was Ephesians 3:20, it reads:

"Now to him who is able to do far more abundantly than all that we ask or think, according to the power at work within us."

That evening Dr. Munroe said changed his life and set him on the path to become one of The Bahamas' leading figures in religion and not only the Bahamas but around the world. His personal life's story of trial and triumph has inspired countless of thousands of people to overcome their own personal trials.

While I can identify many other individuals in many different spheres of leadership who emerged as a result of a personal crisis, I cannot tell their story better than I can tell mine. Having lost both of my parents, while at an early age, and marginalized by society because of that fact alone, I was also diagnosed with a rare blood disorder called Lupus at only 10 years old. My mother had passed away from this disorder and now doctors had stated, I would not live pass eighteen years of age. If you have ever read any of my previous books or heard me speak, maybe you are familiar with my personal crisis and how God turned my tragedy into triumph. Please bear with me, because I never tire of testifying about the fact of what was meant to kill me, caused me to emerge into the leader I am today. When I got that diagnoses I decided to put my life on a different course. Remember Paul, who I quoted in the introduction, as he wrote to his protégé Timothy? Well he stated if anyone wants to be a vessel of honor he must purify himself from that which is unrighteous." I decided to make my life count and give my heart to God. This moment in my life proved to be the launching pad of what my future would look like. God truly touched my life and had my attention, so I decided to dedicate my life to his service and work. While I still have the scars, the marks prove that I went through my personal trial but overcame. My testimony has been shared around different parts of the world and used to encourage thousands of teenagers and young adults. I'm proud to say God has kept me past eighteen years old and I lead one of the fastest growing churches on my island. I always ponder if it had not been for my personal crisis, would I have emerged to be the leader I am today?

You are reading this book right now and may be facing a personal crisis of your own; there may be a burden that you are carrying, a load that is too heavy for you. How you respond to your personal crisis will determine whether you emerge as a victim or a victor. "God uses the bad as transportation to the good He has in store, for those who love Him and are called to his purposes." According to Romans 8:28. I truly believe that storms are setups to place us on the stage, God has for us. When you overcome a national or personal crisis and respond to issues with faith and hope, you will emerge as a leader in your generation. People are willing to follow those who have been through hell but still rise as conquerors. The question to ask whenever you face an overwhelming issue is "God, how can I become the solution to this problem, and help others overcome what I have already triumphed over?"

YOUR BURDEN CREATES YOUR MISSION

Leaders respond to issues out of compassion for others. Jesus Had compassion on us in fact the scriptures state this in Matthew 9:36

> "When he saw the crowds, he had compassion for them, because they were harassed and helpless, like sheep without a shepherd." ESV

Jesus was moved by the needs of the people. That word compassion when you break it down means, "From the gut, or intestines." It was the most intense word the writers could find to describe the deep burden Jesus felt as a result of the state of the people. Leaders often find themselves uncomfortable when others are oppressed. They can't sleep without thinking of how they can provide a solution to the issue. Does this describe you in anyway? Can you think of any present issue that moves you so deeply, that it moves you to action?

YOUR MISSION TELLS YOU WHOM AND WHAT

Jesus knew he was sent to the lost sheep of Israel because of that deep compassion. Maybe there is a need in the company you work for that causes you to be burdened, or it's the state of your countries economic situations, or political state, that burdens you to the place you can't sleep. Are you deeply moved when you see people spiritually lost, in an abusive relationship, or homeless and hungry? God allows you to feel and even empathize with these issues because that burden creates your mission. These are the

5

areas He wants to use you in, to help provide an answer for. You not only have compassion but empathize with others. Maybe you were in an abusive relationship and overcame; help others to do the same. Were you ever homeless or jobless, but created your own business? Show others how to do the same, maybe you were spiritually lost and dying, show others how to find the right path; maybe a teacher gave up on you and your self-esteem was low, yet you overcame, then help those that feel lost, least and left out to find their Mission in life. Do you know the burden of being a Single mother or father? Help others! Every great inventor or invention provided a solution to a problem. I personally have a burden for young people, because God changed my life at a very young age. It moves me deeply when I see a young life headed in the wrong direction and so I made it my mission to reach young people like myself to find their God given purpose, that they were planted on the planet to perform. If you want to emerge as a world class leader begin to find the people and problems God wants you to help bring solutions to. This is what creates that selfless character that all world changing leaders possess. Remember Leaders are vessels, vessels are used to pour. You can't be a leader and selfish, because leaders understand their main purpose is to serve. Leaders ask one question no matter where they are, "How can I help?" Your mission always involves others and it's never all about you. God told Abraham "Through you nations would be blessed" Who is it God, wants to bless through you?

"Being a leader means being able to help others discover and then live out their potential by inspiring them to seek it every day."

- Dan Cathy

YOUR MISSION BECOMES YOUR PASSION

Anything that burdens you will be on your mind constantly, and whenever you help provide a solution for that issue it brings you Joy that no amount of money can ever give you. Your passion is that one thing no one has to pay you to do. Emerging leaders are always those that are passionate about what they pursue. There is a sense of fulfilment that comes to them, because they are doing what it is they were born to do. Millions of people around the world, wake up every day and go through life miserable and frustrated because they go to jobs they don't like, to deal with issues that mean nothing to them, it's just a paycheck. What a sad and shameful state to live life in. The moment you find that one thing that you are passionate about it points you in the direction of purpose. At the end of my life I would feel as if I had finish my course, my mission, my purpose, because I'm doing what I love to do. My life is not mediocre in any sense, every day is a journey, and a new sense of fulfilment every time I pursue my Mission.

"You have to be burning with an idea, or a problem, or a wrong that you want to right. If you're not passionate enough from the start, you'll never stick it out."

— Steve Jobs

"There is no passion to be found playing small--in settling for a life that is less than the one you are capable of living."

-Nelson Mandela

7

THE MAN WHO HAD A BURDEN FOR A BROKEN WALL

I mentioned Nehemiah earlier and promised I would get back to him. His story is one of the most potent and practical ones, we find in scripture that supports this principle. I encourage you to read the book of Nehemiah, even though we will reference it throughout this book. Basically His story starts by telling us he asked a question about how the people that were left in Jerusalem were doing. He got a report that broke his heart and eventually became a burden. The report was the wall was broken that protected the people from danger. As soon as Nehemiah got this report he began to weep, the scriptures state that he goes days in prayer and fasting about the situation he couldn't sleep without thinking about the broken wall, but more than that, the broken people. (Nehemiah 1:1-4)

Nehemiah actually had a great Job and a comfortable life, he was the king's cup bearer, yet this burden drove him to the point that it redirected his life. Sometimes burdens redirect you. You may be majoring in one area in college, but when you discover your burden you may change your major. You may have a successful and bright career in one field, and a burden will, cause you to charter a new courses. That's what took place with Nehemiah, his whole direction in life was interrupted, yet he would emerge as a leader as a result of his burden (Nehemiah 2:1-4)

"What breaks your heart might just be the thing that drives you to change your world." – Andy Stanley

I encourage you to discover your Burden, when you do, it directs you toward your purpose, your mission in life; you become compassionate, empathetic and passionate about following that mission. Ask yourself "What breaks my heart?" Don't settle for a mediocre life! Emerge out of the ashes of your fiery trials and turn your tragedies into triumph. Let your storms set you up for your stage that God has designed for you. Maybe you haven't discovered this Mission yet my prayer is that God will show you even at a young age. I know you're only concerned about finishing high school or college right now, but when a burden hits your heart, that is nothing you can fake and that burden won't let you rest until you see the mission accomplished. Which leads us to the second principle every emerging leader should discover, but before we go there I want you to take some time and write down one or two sentences that describe your mission. For example, my life's mission statement is:

"I exist, to help lead people into a growing relationship with Jesus Christ."

This is what drives me and motivates me every day; I get excited every day God allows me to live, because I get to do what I love to do, my mission.

What's yours? Write it in the space provided below:

DISCOVER YOUR VISION 2

"The only thing worse than being blind, is having sight and no vision."

- Helen Keller

THE DIFFERENCE BETWEEN VISION AND MISSION:

While your Mission is who and what you will reach, your vision says, how you will do that. Vision speaks to your strategy and objectives. Your vision keeps you motivated for the mission. Your Vision will usually have two different levels 1) They will be short term and 2) they will be long term. "What do I see in the near future and what do I see in the distant future." Every Leader that God has ever used to make a lasting difference, did so by having a vision. Martin Luther King Jr. didn't just have a burden he had a vision he stated in one of his most famous speeches "I have a dream..." Jesus had a burden but he also had a vision. Hebrews 12:2 states:

"Looking to Jesus, the founder and perfecter of our faith, who for **the joy that was set before him** endured the cross…"

Jesus saw ahead of him, the Joy that was the reward if he followed through on the burden. The scriptures teach us in Proverbs 29:18 the A clause:

> Where there is no vision, the people perish: but he that keepeth the law, happy is he. KJV

So many people never fulfill their life's mission because they simply never had the vision of where they wanted to go and how they were going to get there. Let's get a working definition for "Vision."

> "Vision is the ability to think about or plan the future with imagination or wisdom. The act or power of anticipating that which will or may come to be"

Vessels are Visionaries, As God pours His Spirit on you He enables you to have vision and wisdom. Joel prophesied it, the disciples experienced it and Peter explained it.

> "For these people are not drunk, as you suppose, since it is only the third hour of the day. But this is what was uttered through the prophet Joel:
> "And in the last days it shall be, God declares, that I will **pour out my Spirit** on all flesh, and your sons and your daughters shall prophesy, and your young men shall **see visions**, and your old men **shall dream dreams**; even on my male servants and female servants
> in those days I will pour out my Spirit, and they shall prophesy."
> Acts 2:15-18 ESV

When you are filled with Gods Spirit you can't help but to be a visionary and a dreamer, because you can see what will be, not just what is.

DREAM OUT LOUD

Visionaries have foresight, they see beyond their present into their potential future. Vision says "My current Position does not have to dictate my future Potential." One of my favorite dreamers or visionaries that I absolutely love is the biblical Joseph. At the age of fourteen God gave Joseph a Dream, a prophetic vision of what was to come in his life. While his current situation didn't seem to match what God was saying Joseph held on to his dreams. Even when others didn't believe in his vision he held on. It's important to understand that not everyone will believe in your dream or vision right away. As a matter of fact most times they will look at who you are and where you are and say it's not possible. I encourage you not to allow what others say or see to dictate your moves, rather allow Gods word to have the final say. If you're not aware of what his plans are I can tell you now, they are to prosper you, to give you a hope a future and expected end. (Jeremiah 29:11)

Josephs brothers didn't believe in his dream, as a matter of fact they were jealous of the favor God had on his life, and conspired to kill him. I can tell you now; I have personally learned what it truly means to dream out loud. Dreaming Loud doesn't mean I tell everyone my dreams, it simply means I allow myself to dream BIG.

"Shoot for the moon and if you miss you will still be among the stars."

- Les Brown

-

I learned this principle of not talking to everyone about my dreams over the years, because there are dream killers, people that will try to kill your vision even before it has time to develop. Nehemiah also faced opposition to the vision God had given him. There were two individuals in particular that were very dogmatic and condescending toward His efforts. They set out to discourage the people. These dream killers highlighted their weaknesses and asked will they really be able to fix what is broken? (Nehemiah 7) Yet Nehemiah never allowed them to highjack his hope.

I have also discovered that when God has a plan for your life, nothing or no one can stop it. Josephs' brothers thought, by throwing him in a pit and selling him as a slave would have stopped Gods plans, but they only positioned him for the plan. The only person that can press pause on your potential future is yourself. That's if you stop believing and if you stop pursuing your dreams, because of the nay sayers. If everyone could see the things God has shown you then everybody would have already been doing it. That's what makes a world class leader, one that is a cut above the rest, the ability to see beyond the present into the potential future. It can get lonely at the top, but if you stick with the vision, it won't be long before other people start to see it and eventually join it. So follow your dreams, it may not be easy but in the end it will be worth it. Joseph made a powerful statement at the conclusion of his story. His brothers wanted to apologize for trying to kill what God had shown him, and for how they handled him and here is what the scriptures record Joseph as saying:

You intended to harm me, **but God intended it all for good**. He brought me to this position so I could **save the lives of many people**. Genesis

50:20 NLT

After all when your vision is connected to providing solutions to a burden, helping others to find their potential and purpose, God will preserve you. In a great House there are vessels of honor and those are the ones you preserve until they have completed their assignment. Dream Out Loud!

"Purpose is when you know and understand what you were born to accomplish. Vision is when you see it in your mind and begin to imagine it"

-   Dr. Myles Munroe

GIFTED FOR THE VISION

God has planted in you the gift and the resources you need to fulfill your mission. One of the hindrances that stop people from following their dream is the feelings of fear and being incapable of achieving what they set out to achieve. Believe me I can tell you there was so many times I questioned myself, or felt unqualified to do what God was showing me. When I faced a crisis within the denomination I was apart of for most of my teenage years and vocation as a full time minister, the situation basically forced my wife and I to have to make a hard decision, to go out on our own. This was not an easy decision and it came with much prayer and fasting. As we sought God for the next step for our lives, there was this constant burden to stay on the island we currently reside, at the time of writing this book, and start a nondenominational ministry. We had a deep burden and saw a need for a church that would reach a generation of young adults that most traditional churches were not reaching. No matter how we tried to shake it and make the most convenient and safe choice for our future, the burden was too heavy. As we started to make plans to follow Gods direction, there was this sense of fear and inadequacy; I was going crazy with voices speaking in my head, not outside ones, but my own internal fears. I started to question my ability to start and lead a church effectively, I didn't know where provision for my family would come from initially and our personal savings would only last us for so long. I was 29 years of age and had a growing family depending on me. Deep inside regardless of my internal wars and fears, I believe if God gave me the vision, he would make the provision, and where I was inadequate he would become sufficient. Sharai and I stepped out on faith, and did not allow our fears to pause what God wanted us to do. Two years later and now Relevant Kingdom Center has become one of the fastest growing churches, in Exuma. We have had countless testimonies of how God has moved in people's lives and how they have been set free from what held them hostage. As time went on God gave me wisdom that I didn't even know I had, until I was faced with making decisions and providing the necessary direction, for a church. As a result, I have also been able to discover hidden abilities that I would have never discovered had I not stepped out in faith. It has not been easy, but it has been worth it. God had also placed men and women in our lives, who believed in the vision and dream, they believed in my God given abilities and helped to finance the dream. The first year a couple decided they would assist with our living arrangements and allowed me to stay in their apartment absolutely free of charge. The only thing I had to take care of was my electricity bill. Shortly after another couple decided they would support us financially, until the church was able to support us fully, even to this day they still sow into our lives on a consistent basis. The God of the Vision will provide! When God gives you a burden, he will give you a vision and make the necessary provision. Don't allow fear or even your own flaws to stop you from following your dream

.

"Remember what God originates he will also Orchestrate!" – Andy Stanley

Do I feel worthy to be used? Not at all, yet my trust rest in God and His grace. The Apostle Paul didn't feel worthy, he had issues yet he became one of Gods greatest vessels of all time. I have discovered that God is an awesome architect and a divine designer. The bible describes heaven with streets made of gold, rivers flowing with milk and honey and the gates made with pearls. However, I asked myself why didn't God, when He made man, make us from gold or platinum or even silver? Yet he decided to make us from dirt! I then realized that you can't plant a seed in gold, or any other precious substance, dirt is the most conducive and effective environment for a seed. And God has placed a gift (a Seed) within us. Biologist has also discovered that the human body is 60- 70% water. So when you have dirt, seed and water, it equals produce! Everything you need to be productive lies within you and all you have to do is stick with what God has shown you.

SPIDER SENSE FOR THE VISION

Solomon one of the wisest men to ever walk on the face of the earth made this observation and encouraged us to do the same:

"The spider taketh hold with her hands, and is in kings' palaces."
- Proverbs 30:28 KJV

Spiders are unique creatures, God created them with everything they needed within them. As a matter of fact they make their homes from what's within them, they nourish themselves by what is within them, they move from place to place all by what is on the inside of them. If the spider never uses what God has placed within them, they would bring death to themselves. Solomon observed that the spider even ends up within the Kings palace as a result of what's within them. I want you to know there is a gift within you and that gift will help you achieve your vision.

"A man's gift makes room for him and brings him before the great."
- Proverbs 18:16 ESV
-

Your gift when you allow it to be used, like the spider will land you in the presence of Kings. Dr. Munroe came from, humble beginnings, when he allowed what God said over his life to dictate his vision for his life and not the teacher that didn't believe in his dream; he ended up in the palaces of kings. Before he passed away, many Government Leaders, Kings and Prime Ministers, C.E.Os of major corporations, consulted him. All because he allowed what was in him to come out. My gift has taken me places I never imagined I would go. It has paid for tickets, I could have never afforded and allowed my family and I do to do things we could have never done. Had I not allowed my spider sense to kick in, and release the gift within me, none of that would have been posible. What are your spider senses telling you? What gifts are you allowing to lay dormant because you feel inadequate or unworthy? Activate your gifts so you can fulfill your mission though your vision.

SACRIFICE FOR THE VISION

Vision will always call for sacrifice and no person that is unwilling to make a sacrifice; will ever truly be a leader that makes history. Sacrifice is at the heart of leadership. You will have to give up what you like for what you love, the immediate for the ultimate. As young emerging leaders we can forget that nothing comes over night. We live in a fast food mentality, society. We want everything now and we want it fast. Success comes over time and that time involves a lot of sacrifice. I remember when Sharia and I first left Freeport to reside on the island we are currently, at the time of writing this book. It was a difficult decision to leave what we were used to, and to be honest what we were comfortable with. We had just completed a brand new home, every young couples dream; my wife had just given birth to our fourth son Dashaun and we had a vibrant youth ministry.

Doors were opening in a huge way for us and God was truly increasing my influence. I travelled to Exuma on a speaking engagement at the time for one of my former denominations churches, at the time they were looking for a Pastor to carry on the work that had recently started and immediately after I came and spoke I was asked to consider taking up the post as the lead pastor. I must tell you that Exuma, for my wife and I wasn't the most desirable destination. While it is picture perfect, with beautiful waters and incredible people, the island isn't that big and there was a lack of conveniences that we were used to. No fast foods, social outings, such as movie theaters or bowling alleys. We had no family and would have to develop new friendships. There is also a lack of emergency health care and options for education, as opposed to Freeport or Nassau, so it was a sacrificial decision for persons in their late 20's early 30's to make.

Regardless of all I mentioned above; I would also have to explain to our youth leaders and ministry that I was going to pack my bags and leave in order to go to an island I knew absolutely nothing about. I knew many of them wouldn't understand why we would leave, and others were heartbroken that we did. I did have a choice on whether to leave or not and at first decided I would assist with the church by commuting back and forth every weekend. The commute called for long exhausting trips every time. However, it was all God's plan to set me up for where we are now. The more I came to Exuma the more my heart felt burdened for the people, and the more I felt the burden the more needs I saw unmet. There was a breach in the wall, and the postmodern generation that did call the island their home, didn't seem to have much relevant ministry that impacted them. Sharai and I prayed about it and finally decided to leave everything we had worked so hard for behind, including our brand new home! It has not been easy at all but as we see the lives changed as a result of our obedience, we know it is worth it. Since moving, every year we found ourselves in different apartments or homes, trying to find the right place to settle until God directs us otherwise; we left a stable one for an unsure one. We know the future will call for more sacrifices. If you truly want to be a history maker prepare to make sacrifices.

A noble purpose inspires sacrifice, stimulates innovation and encourages

19

perseverance.

-   Gary Hamel

Nelson Mandela South Africa's first black Chief Executive, sacrificed for what he was passionate about and spent 27 years in prison. Confined to a small cell, the floor his bed, a bucket for a toilet, he was forced to do hard labor. He gave up immediate pleasure for his ultimate purpose. Many civil rights activists gave up freedoms and made sacrifices all because of their passion and vision. Philosopher – poet, Ralph Waldo Emerson observed, *"For everything you have missed, you have gained something else, and for everything you gain, you lose something."*

'Life is a series of trades, one thing for another." Leaders must give up, going up. That's the true of every leader regardless of profession. Talk to leaders, and you will find that they have made repeated sacrifices. Effective leaders sacrifice much that is good in order to dedicate them to what is best. That's how the principle of sacrifice works. Nehemiah had to sacrifice the luxuries of the king's palace, to go to the arduous task of rebuilding a broken wall. Jesus sacrificed his life just so that he could fulfill his mission in a deprived world. As he gathered his followers, those that would go on to turn the world upside down and make history, He repeatedly reminded them of the great sacrifices they would have to make. Many of whom lost their lives for the sake of the gospel and the burden of seeing a dying world receives life and life more abundantly. When you become a leader you lose the right to think of yourself alone because of the great responsibility of leadership.

Then he said to the crowd, "If any of you wants to be my follower, you must turn from your selfish ways, take up your cross daily, and follow me.

-Luke 9:23 NLT

How does this apply to leaders in other fields? If you're in business and desire to start your own company, it may call for you not taking a salary for yourself for some time. If you desire to go in the medical field, you must be prepared for long years and hours of intense study, and sacrifice, if you're an athlete that desires a professional spot in your field, it will mean spending time disciplining yourself in your area of expertise, no matter what field what area of influence it will always call for a sacrifice. Remember, "You have to be willing to give up on the way up."

FOCUS ON THE VISION

As Paul continued to encourage his young protégé Timothy, an emerging leader, he encouraged him to activate his gifts. He didn't stop there he told him to practice, cultivate and develop his gifts 1Timothy 4:13-15. Your vision helps to provide focus to your life. A person without vision will go in different directions every day but when you have vision you set your course and don't allow yourself to veer off for no reason. This principle has helped me to simplify my life. I don not do everything; I focus on my strengths and gifts and maximize those areas of my life more than anything else. My mission is "To lead people into a growing relationship with Jesus." Every day I cultivate my God given abilities so that I can see that mission and vision a reality. I practice, meditate and discipline myself to stay focus on my calling. The problem with doing too much is you can find yourself getting nowhere. If you simplify your life and only do those things that help you

21

accomplish your goals, you will get further faster.

"There are many things I can do, but I have to narrow it down to the one thing I must do. The secret of concentration is elimination."

- Andy Stanley
-

Vision is so full of focus, that if we were to write it down, simplify it so much to the mission at hand, if someone were to pick that written vision up and start to read it, they would be able to accomplish it even though, the vision didn't start with them. God told an Old Testament prophet by the name of Habakkuk:

"And the LORD answered me, and said, write the vision, and make it plain upon tables, that he may run that readeth it." Habakkuk 2:2 KJV

And as you cultivate and focus on the vision don't get weary or distracted because you don't see the results you may want right away, because every vision is for an appointed time. God will bring some to pass in short times, but other times the vision is for a distant future. God knows the timing as long as you remain committed and focused; he will bring it to pass (Habakkuk 2:3).

Nehemiah was approached to stop doing what he was commissioned to do, which was build the wall, but he had such bulldog focus that he refused to stop working on his goal. His statement was so potent that I decided just to place it below as a quote that stands out on its own.

"I am doing a great work and I cannot come down."

Nehemiah 6:2 ESV

Your vision is to great, too much will be at stake for you to lose your focus.

GET CREATIVE WITH THE VISION

Steve Jobs in my opinion was one of the 21st century's most creative minds. His simple approach to life and business helped him to maximize his imagination. He had a vision for technology, and was focused on that vision. If you walk in any apple store or use any apple product you are amazed by its capabilities, but yet its simplicity. The more focused you are, the more creative you can become. What has allowed me to step out of the box of mediocrity is the unwavering focus I have to my mission. We are so focused in what we do, that every day we look for new, innovative ways to do it. For example, some Sundays when I speak I don't simply go up on the stage with a speech, but we have backdrops, illustrations, props, videos and so much more that help us in our vision. People are attracted to creativity. Creative leaders aren't afraid to do what others are not willing to try. Even in the face of failure, creativity pushes you beyond your comfort zone and helps you to develop your gift and skill, to become more effective in reaching the mission

"Creativity is putting your imagination to work, and it's produced the most extraordinary results in human culture."

- Ken Robinson

Remember vision involves imagination. Allow yourself to imagine, to develop concepts the world has yet to see, or things that would take your field or sphere of influence to another level.

23

DUERRE AND SHARAI THOMAS

Vision calls for risk, risk calls for courage and creativity involves both, risk and courage.

"Focus and simplicity. Simple can be harder than complex: You have to work hard to get your thinking clean to make it simple. But it's worth it in the end because once you get there, you can move mountains."

- Steve Jobs

I am committed to allowing myself to dream out loud. I have a determination to use the gifts God placed inside me and refuse to allow my own fears and flaws, to press pause on my potential. I trust that if my vision originates from God, He will also orchestrate it. Emerging leaders have to activate and cultivate their God given gifts. It requires commitment and focus. In that regard, I have come up with not just a mission statement for my life, but a vision statement:

"I will use my ability to speak and write in a creative way to reach people far from God and lead them into a growing relationship with Jesus."

What's your Vision statement? Remember the Mission is the "What" and the Vision is the "How."

DISCOVER YOUR PLAN

3

"Leadership is the capacity to translate vision into reality."

—Warren Bennis

EVERY LEADER NEEDS A PLAN

When Nehemiah followed his burden and responded to his vision in faith, amazingly enough he didn't just immediately go to work. Once he arrived to Jerusalem the first thing he did was go out to survey the damage and come up with a plan. I'll let Nehemiah explain what he did.

11 So I went to Jerusalem and was there three days. 12 Then I arose in the night, I and a few men with me. And I told no one what my God had put into my heart to do for Jerusalem. There was no animal with me but the one on which I rode. 13 I went out by night by the Valley Gate to the Dragon Spring and to the Dung Gate, and I inspected the walls of Jerusalem that were broken down and its gates that had been destroyed by fire. 14 Then I went on to the Fountain Gate and to the King's Pool, but there was no room for the animal that was under me to pass. 15 Then I went up in the night by the valley and inspected the wall, and I turned back and entered by the Valley Gate, and so returned. 16 And the officials did not know where I had gone or what I was doing, and I had

not yet told the Jews, the priests, the nobles, the officials, and the rest who were to do the work.

17 Then I said to them, "You see the trouble we are in, how Jerusalem lies in ruins with its gates burned. Come, let us build the wall of Jerusalem, that we may no longer suffer derision." 18 And I told them of the hand of my God that had been upon me for good, and also of the words that the king had spoken to me. And they said, "Let us rise up and build." So they strengthened their hands for the good work.

- Nehemiah 2:11-17 ESV

-

This was such an amazing strategy. First he never told anyone what was on his heart "the vision" until he came up with a plan. In fact people didn't even know what he was doing; while they were sleeping he was planning. I realize that great leaders, don't sleep when others are, they're too busy planning for their purpose. I'm not suggesting you do not rest, I am suggesting that planning takes time and wisdom. People follow leaders that have a strategy and a plan. This principle is carried over into the business world all the time. If you go to the bank or an investor, to fund your vision, they usually ask for a business plan. They want to see that you have taken the time to think things through. Many times, as young emerging leaders we get excited and anxious, and while our vision may be great, our planning isn't. We rush into things without considering the cost and surveying our situations, we overlook things that are detrimental to our vision. Here is what Jesus taught in scripture:

28 For which of you, desiring to build a tower, does not first sit down and count the cost, whether he has enough to complete it? 29 Otherwise, when he has laid a foundation and is not able to finish, all who see it begin to mock him, 30 saying, 'This man began to build and was not able

to finish.'

- Luke 14:28-29 ESV

I believe that every great vision takes faith to respond, but I also believe that faith is not foolish as most of us have been taught. When we stepped out and started the church, before we ever launched out, I first surveyed the situation came up with a strategy, developed the plan and then communicated that plan. When people heard and saw that we took time to think things though they stood up and strengthened their hands and hearts for the work that was ahead. To this day I sit down in November of every year, and strategize and plan for what I believe God has placed on my heart. I offer my plans to God and trust him to give me the wisdom on how to follow through. Planning doesn't indicate a lack of faith, planning actually compliments faith. Faith and planning are not contradictory but complementary. As I sit and write even now, my heart is stirred on the importance of planning. To the point I'm reminded that even God plans. I mentioned this scripture in our previous chapter but I believe it bears repeating here

For I know the plans I have for you, declares the Lord, plans for welfare[a] and not for evil, to give you a future and a hope.

- Jeremiah 29:11

God states, I have planned your future and your life! I have taken time to think of what I will do for you even before you were born. Jeremiah, an Old Testament prophet fully understood this and this scripture has become one of my favourite themes.

"Before I formed you in the womb I knew you,

DUERRE AND SHARAI THOMAS

and before you were born I consecrated you;
I appointed you a prophet to the nations." -Jeremiah 1:5

Every great leader did not accidently land in greatness they planned to be positioned in greatness.

PATHS ARE CREATED BY A PLAN

"Your direction ultimately determines your destination." – Andy Stanley

Now that we have discussed the importance of having a plan, let's get a working definition on what a plan is:

"It is a written account of intended future course of action (scheme) aimed at achieving specific goal(s) or objective(s) within a specific timeframe."

The plan then is really a detailed written strategy, of how you will accomplish your Vision. It is like the blueprint for a carpenter to follow in order to achieve the desired results of the visionary, the architect. God is the Architect of our lives and He has the plans already written down, it's up to us to strengthen our hands and hearts for the work and follow the details of the plan. Scripture tells us, "Many are the plans of a man's heart, but it is always Gods purposes that prevail in the end." (Proverbs 19:21). No wonder Nehemiah spent so much time in prayer and seeking God, because he didn't go to Jerusalem with his own agenda, he went with the plans from the Architect of life, God Himself. God's plans never fail and it's important for us to seek God for His plans because they provide direction to us, they help create the paths we follow. When we veer off track and do what seems right in our own eyes, we delay reaching our desired goals and destination. Another metaphor to what this plan looks like is a map. Maps are detailed outlined directions that tell you how to get from one point to the next. So if you are planning for your vision, it is the strategy that tells you what you will do and how you will do it, what steps you will make and each step, should lead you closer to your destination. What's amazing is we have digital maps or GPS systems, these kinds of maps give you distance and tells you how long it will take you to reach a particular point. When you sit down and plan, make sure you write down how long it will take and when you want to see certain things take place. Remember, everything is in Gods time and sometimes our plans don't turn out like we expect them to.

YOU CAN ADJUST A PLAN

"Failed plans should not be interpreted as a failed vision. Visions don't change, they are only refined. Plans rarely stay the same, and are scrapped or adjusted as needed. Be stubborn about the vision, but flexible with your plan."

- John C. Maxwell

There were many times in my life and in my drive to follow the burden and vision, I realized certain plans just didn't seem to work. As a result I had to be flexible enough, to change the plans but stick to the vision. Plans, at times, are met with unexpected stops and blocks, but no matter what don't think your vision has failed just look at new ways to adjust the plan to help you land in the desired destination. Nehemiah as he was building the wall had to make adjustments as they progressed. Of course the dream killers, created opposition that tried to hinder them from finishing the wall and when they saw the Jews were close to accomplishing their vision, the enemy started to plan (Nehemiah 4:7-8). Isn't that amazing, that even the enemy plans? The devil is strategizing how he will discourage you from the vision, and when your plans are met with disappointment, it makes you feel depressed, drained and frustrated, until finally you throw in the towel. The burden you had the heart to respond to ends up becoming a load too heavy for you to bear, and you get burnt out and tired. Let's read what took place and how Nehemiah was flexible enough to adjust the Plan, but stick to the vision, even when others were encouraging them to quit:

In Judah it was said, "The strength of those who bear the burdens is failing. There is too much rubble. By ourselves we will not be able to rebuild the wall." 11 And our enemies said, "They will not know or see till we come among them and kill them and stop the work." 12 At that time the Jews who lived near them came from all directions and said to us ten times, "You must return to us." 13 So in the lowest parts of the space behind the wall, in open places, I stationed the people by their clans, with their swords, their spears, and their bows. 14 And I looked and arose and said to the nobles and to the officials and to the rest of the people, "Do not be afraid of them. Remember the Lord, who is great and awesome, and fight for your brothers, your sons, your daughters, your wives, and your homes."

15 When our enemies heard that it was known to us and that **God had frustrated their plan,** we all returned to the wall, each to his work. 16 From that day on, half of my servants worked on construction, and half

held the spears, shields, bows, and coats of mail. And the leaders stood behind the whole house of Judah, 17 who were building on the wall. Those who carried burdens were loaded in such a way that each labored on the work with one hand and held his weapon with the other. 18 And each of the builders had his sword strapped at his side while he built.

When you keep working the vision and remain steadfast regardless of the unexpected opposition to your plans, it frustrates the enemy. This is the tenacity that all great leaders have, they refuse to quit, even when it seemed the plan wouldn't work. Their Experience now caused Nehemiah to use wisdom. He made the necessary adjustments and continued the work.

"Anytime you suffer a setback or disappointment, put your head down and plow ahead."

\- Les Brown

"I advise you to say your dream is possible and then overcome all inconveniences, ignore all the hassles and take a running leap through the hoop, even if it is in flames."

\- Les Brown

Are you ready to Plan? Have you taken the time to sit down and discover your plan? It is the road map, the blueprint on how to reach the Vision and fulfil the mission. Take time as we end this chapter to seek Gods face for the next 3 days. Ask God to give you wisdom beyond your years, and strategies to take the steps that lead you closer to your vision. If you have already gotten a plan in mind, it's still not a plan until it's written down, make it clear and precise and even put a time frame on when you look to reach certain milestones. For the ministry I lead, we are in the process of looking for a permanent home, land and building, I have decided to build the plans even before I get the land or see the spot, because my Faith, what I foresee compliments the plans I have made. I have written this down and placed the statement "Within five years" we hope to be in our own building." Gods timing is not mine, it can be sooner and it can be later, but it will not be that I failed to plan.

DISCOVER YOUR VALUES 4

"Character is doing the right thing when nobody's looking. There are too many people who think that the only thing that's right is to get by, and the only thing that's wrong is to get caught."

J.C. Watts

CHARACTER OVER CHARISMA

While your gifts and talents will make room for you, *Character* is what keeps you there. People are inspired by trust worthy leadership; those that hold up standards in their lives. It's ok to have a dynamic personality, and to be gifted and talented, but a leader without character or integrity is a leader destined for failure! Your charisma or "wonderful" personality will attract people to you, but your *character* will keep them following you! The current problem we face in today's society is that we tend to overlook what *is* good for what *looks* good! While appearances do have a part to play, it's the heart that matters most to God!

But the Lord said to Samuel, "Don't judge by his appearance or height, for I have rejected him. The Lord doesn't see things the way you see them. People judge by outward appearance, but the Lord looks at the heart."

- 1 Samuel 16:7 (NLT)

In this same passage of scripture, David was about to be chosen by God to be anointed as king. The prophet Samuel was sent by God to David's house to anoint a new king. As David was out doing his chores, his brothers lined up before Samuel as he inspected each kingly candidate, he was sure God would approve of one of them! After all, each one was well built and handsome and looked like kingly material! But to Samuel's surprise God refused every last one and had David chosen above the rest! Samuel was so focused on the outward appearance of David's brothers that God had to put him in check!

God said it's the heart that matters most to me! Isn't that like some of us? We can easily become so overly concerned by the superficial, by the exterior, by what looks good to us that we miss out on what matters most to God! As Leaders, God will judge us not by how well we performed but how well we lived!

"It is true that integrity alone won't make you a leader, but without integrity you will never be one."

-Zig Ziglar

As David's story continues we find that he was loved by many and praised for his accomplishments and victories, but he soon learned that maintaining his *integrity* or character was the *key* to his success as a leader!

One evening David got up from his bed and walked around on the roof of the palace. From the roof he saw a woman bathing. The woman was very beautiful, [3] and David sent someone to find out about her. The man said, "She is Bathsheba, the daughter of Eliam and the wife of Uriah the

Hittite." ⁴ Then David sent messengers to get her. She came to him, and he slept with her. Then she went back home. ⁵ The woman conceived and sent word to David, saying, "I am pregnant."

-2 Samuel 11:1-5

In the morning David wrote a letter to Joab and sent it with Uriah. ¹⁵ In it he wrote, "Put Uriah out in front where the fighting is fiercest. Then withdraw from him so he will be struck down and die."
¹⁶ So while Joab had the city under siege, he put Uriah at a place where he knew the strongest defenders were. ¹⁷ When the men of the city came out and fought against Joab, some of the men in David's army fell; moreover, Uriah the Hittite died.

-2 Samuel 11:14-17

Can you imagine after all the victories won for the kingdom, after all the praise and applause and love shown to David by the people, after all the blessings God bestowed upon David and his house; he neglected the most important thing a Leader should have, for the sake of charisma? Let's define this word *Integrity!*

Integrity originates from the Latin word *integritas,* which means *whole; or undivided*!!

When placed in context, that means our lives should not be divided into parts or compartmentalized, but each area of our lives should be upheld by the same standard; for a believer our standard should be God's Word! So, what you see is what you get! I'm no *hypocrite* because who I am in public is who I am in private!

If our whole heart truly belongs to Him, then we must apply His word to *every* area of our lives, and not just a part of it! His word will definitely challenge the areas of our life that we struggle in, but if we submit our desires to Him and allow God to take control, we will be more productive in our life and He will be able to use us so much more!

David learned this the hard way and he went against his own values and violated the principles God had set in place as a safe guard, not realizing that his children would have to live with the decisions he made in private; decisions that eventually became public and affected everyone in the kingdom!

Why did you despise the word of the Lord by doing what is evil in his eyes? You struck down Uriah the Hittite with the sword and took his wife to be your own. You killed him with the sword of the Ammonites. [10] Now, therefore, the sword will never depart from your house, because you despised me and took the wife of Uriah the Hittite to be your own.'
[11] "This is what the Lord says: 'Out of your own household I am going to bring calamity on you. Before your very eyes I will take your wives and give them to one who is close to you, and he will sleep with your wives in broad daylight. [12] You did it in secret, but I will do this thing in broad daylight before all Israel.'"

- 2 Samuel 12: 9-12

When you assume the role or take on the position of a leader, your life isn't your own anymore! Growing up as a pastor's kid and as the first-born child, I knew this all too well and as a result, there were many expectations placed on me as I grew up! Even though I had so many pleasant moments in my childhood, and even though I gave my life to God and had a personal relationship with Jesus Christ, I began to resent that my life was lived in a "glass house"! I resented some of the rules and restrictions placed on me by my parents, not always acknowledging the fact they were there to protect my character!

As an emerging leader God takes you from the shelf of life, and places you on the stage of life to be a display for the world to see! It wasn't until I matured in my faith and thinking, that I understood the privilege and honor it was to be *called out* by God; to be set on a stage to bring glory to Him through my life! I then realized that as a leader not only did I have people looking at me, but I had many people looking up to me and imitating me.

I want to lead with integrity, to lift my head with a sense of pride and self-respect, to not only make others proud, but God proud! So if you find yourself frustrated as a leader because of the expectations placed on you, just remember if you trust and rely upon God to lead you, you will receive the grace to carry the load and do what He's called you to do! You will feel fulfilled knowing you made an impact on someone's life and future, and maybe even on generations to come! It's all for the glory of God!

"If I take care of my character, my reputation will take care of me."

-Dwight L. Moody

THE HUMBLE HEART

Pride is an independent, me-oriented spirit. It makes people arrogant, rude and hard to get along with. When our heart is prideful, we don't give God the credit and we mistreat people, looking down on them and thinking we deserve what we have.   – Joyce Myer

The Bible describes humility in Colossians 3:12, as meekness or lowliness and being absent of self. Humility is not about an outward show or appearance of humility. Anyone can put on a show like the religious elite in Jesus' day and still have a heart full of arrogance and pride, but remember it's the heart that matters most to God! When we come before God as sinners he requires that we humble ourselves before him, knowing and acknowledging that we are spiritually empty without Him!

Humility isn't only necessary to get into the Kingdom of heaven, but to be great in the Kingdom as well! (Matthew 20:26-27) Jesus was the greatest example of a leader who showed humility! When Jesus came to this earth he didn't come to be served, but to serve others! Though He was God made flesh, he humbled himself and taught others how to lead by placing others above yourself! He is our ultimate example of *True Leadership* and we should pay close attention to the examples he has given to us as a blueprint!

Paul is also to be our example of humility. In spite of the great gifts and understanding he had received, Paul saw himself as the "least of the apostles", and the worst of sinners! (1Corinthians 15:9)

It truly takes a great leader to express genuine humility, especially when he has great affluence and authority over much!

Then David said to Nathan, "I have sinned against the Lord." Nathan replied, "The Lord has taken away your sin. You are not going to die. 14 But because by doing this you have shown utter contempt for[a] the Lord, the son born to you will die." After Nathan had gone home, the Lord struck the child that Uriah's wife had borne to David, and he became ill. 16 David pleaded with God for the child. He fasted and spent the nights lying in sackcloth[b] on the ground. 17 The elders of his household stood beside him to get him up from the ground, but he refused, and he would not eat any food with them.

[18] On the seventh day the child died. David's attendants were afraid to tell him that the child was dead, for they thought, "While the child was still living, he wouldn't listen to us when we spoke to him. How can we now tell him the child is dead? He may do something desperate."
[19] David noticed that his attendants were whispering among themselves, and he realized the child was dead. "Is the child dead?" he asked.
"Yes," they replied, "he is dead."
[20] Then David got up from the ground. After he had washed, put on lotions and changed his clothes, he went into the house of the Lord and worshiped. Then he went to his own house, and at his request they served him food, and he ate.
[21] His attendants asked him, "Why are you acting this way? While the child was alive, you fasted and wept, but now that the child is dead, you get up and eat!"
[22] He answered, "While the child was still alive, I fasted and wept. I thought, 'Who knows? The Lord may be gracious to me and let the child live.' [23] But now that he is dead, why should I go on fasting? Can I bring him back again? I will go to him, but he will not return to me."

-2 Samuel 12:13-23

After David's sin was exposed, God took his child from him as punishment because of his sin. David instead of allowing his heart to grow cold and bitter towards God reacted the total opposite! He humbled himself before God and worshipped God! He didn't curse God or turn away from following Him. Instead he repented even though he still suffered and his decision would affect generations after him. I am thankful to know that God gives grace to the Humble and forgives us when we turn from our wrong! (1Peter 5:5). As you emerge into the leader God wants, don't let selfish ambition motivate, but a selfless mission direct your decisions. No matter how much your influence increases, remain humble!

DISCOVER YOUR CONFIDENCE

5

"You gain strength, courage, and confidence by every experience in which you really stop to look fear in the face. You are able to say to yourself, 'I lived through this horror. I can take the next thing that comes along."

- Eleanor Roosevelt

We have discovered our burden points to purpose; vision keeps us focused and values keep us honorable. When we apply these principles we will walk in a godly confidence, which every god fearing leader should have. Be confident in who you are, don't let anyone look down on you because of your youth. Don't let fear hinder you from walking in the confidence you need to have. People love confident leaders. Confidence is what actually set David to walk on the stage of his influence. When everyone else was afraid to face the philistine giant, David a young shepherd boy, decided to stand up against him and people around him was impressed by his Confidence. However there was one person that confused David's confidence with arrogance, lets read the short account of who that was:

But when David's oldest brother, Eliab, heard David talking to the men, he was angry. "What are you doing around here anyway?" he demanded. "What about those few sheep you're supposed to be taking care of? I know about your pride and deceit. You just want to see the battle!" 1 Samuel 17:28

David's own brother thought David was cocky pompous and prideful, however David's pride wasn't in him, his Confidence was in His God. He didn't look at himself as good, but he understood he served a God that was good. He recounted how God kept him in the past and as a result he believed God would be with him in his present. Confidence is different from arrogance; I have been around people who I know were confident and had my fair share of those who wore arrogant. People don't follow arrogance they follow confidence. How do we tell the difference? Below I will do my best to give you different traits of each

ARROGANCE
- ✓ View themselves as superior
- ✓ Always know what's better for others
- ✓ Never seeks advice or council.
- ✓ Never admit their mistakes
- ✓ Revel in the blunders of others

CONFIDENCE
- ✓ Believe in themselves and in their god given abilities
- ✓ Are willing to learn and grow
- ✓ Always seek council and Advice
- ✓ Aren't afraid to admit their mistakes
- ✓ Desire to see others succeed

The truth is however, all of us will have to be careful not to allow pride and arrogance in our hearts especially when God is using us. One of the greatest examples in scripture about how a leader allowed their gift and position to make them arrogant was Saul. Saul had an arrogant Syndrome, even though he started with humility. When God starts to open doors for you, and people begin to recognize your gifts; if you don't stay grounded you will find yourself off course from becoming the leader God expects.

SAUL'S SYNDROME

Saul's Issue came about when he refused to heed the advice and council of God through the prophet Samuel. As king, Saul found himself facing an overwhelming Philistine army with his soldiers deserting him. He looked to Samuel for guidance. Samuel told him to wait for seven days and he would come and offer a sacrifice to ensure God's favor. In hastiness, he did not wait but offered the sacrifice himself fearing an imminent Philistine attack (lack of faith). Thus, Saul did not find favor with the Lord; and though He had given him victory, yet the Lord "sought out a man after his own heart" to later replace Saul as king. That man we know as King David. When David faced Goliath and won, people started to recognize David's Victories and as a result of Saul's arrogance he was intimidated at anyone that threatened his position as king. Eventually David spends 15 years hiding from Saul's anger and jealousy and anyone who supported David, Saul viewed as an enemy. Leaders that have Saul's syndrome protect their positions until they die, they never pass on what God has placed in them, and they become selfish and not selfless. Dr. Myles Munroe, spent many of his teachings encouraging Leaders to die empty, in-fact one of his last messages included a statement that Leaders should always look to pass the baton. The Spirit of the Lord eventually departed from Saul and he was destroyed by his own hand.

In contrast the Apostle Paul was confident, but he was far from arrogant. Paul was used to establish more churches than any other apostle. He had incredible revelations of God's word and wrote over two thirds of the New Testament, yet he had a spirit of humility which set him apart. He held a high approach to his calling but kept a common touch. He understood principles that made him a healthy leader with the God kind of confidence.

> [3] For we are the circumcision, who worship by the Spirit of God[b] and glory in Christ Jesus and put no confidence in the flesh Though I myself have reason for confidence in the flesh also. If anyone else thinks he has reason for confidence in the flesh, I have more: [5] circumcised on the eighth day, of the people of Israel, of the tribe of Benjamin, a Hebrew of Hebrews; as to the law, a Pharisee; [6] as to zeal, a persecutor of the church; as to righteousness under the law,[c] blameless. [7] But whatever gain I had, I counted as loss for the sake of Christ. Philippians 3:3-6

WHAT PRODUCES HEALTHY CONFIDENCE?

"Before you are a leader, success is all about growing yourself. When you become a leader, success is all about growing others." — Jack Welch

Healthy confidence is produced when we take the focus completely off of us and place it on God. It's all about Him receiving Glory and not about us. Our desire should be that when others see what we do, they don't acknowledge us they glorify Him. When we seek to have recognition from others and make it all about producing a name for ourselves, then you become your greatest enemy, you develop Saul's Syndrome. You will look at everyone as a threat to you, and all your life will become is a big self-centered wreck.

Pastor Craig Groschel a Lead Pastor of one of America's largest churches, Lifechurch.tv helps to identify three mindsets that are pervasive with leaders. The first is the mindset **to 1) Make a name and a living for myself**. This level is all about "Me" and "I" believe as a result of "my" skills "I'm good!" at this level I get security and confidence in what I have and what I accumulate and everyone around me becomes an enemy. While making a living is necessary, you should progress from this mindset. Remember we said burden produces passion and passion is something noone has to pay you to do. It's not about how much money I make the kind of car I drive or the clothing I wear. When I'm passionate about something I am compelled, moved to do it. This leads to the second and most common mindset, especially for leaders that are living out their passion and have responded to the thing that breaks their heart the most and that is **2) I want to make a Difference**. By default a lot of passionate leaders live here. It's not about me; I want to make a difference for God. At this level we don't believe "I" am good, but instead start to believe that "We are good." Unfortunately we can feel as if everyone else is not significant, just those that are a part of our stage; those that work in our organization or field are the only ones that can make a difference. With this mindset we make others feel as if their cause is not significant. We get in competition rather than asking how we can compliment others without not just those within. The third and final mindset Craig addresses **is 3) We move from I am good and We are good and recognize "God is good,"** now our confidence moves from believing we are the reason for our success and progress and we place our confidence in God alone. This is where real humility kicks in! I understand I am gifted and that God has a plan, but I am humbled because He didn't have to use me to emerge as a leader. I don't have to do what I'm doing, I get to do what I'm doing and I'm grateful that I can be used for Gods glory. People at this level help to Make History!

Healthy confidence is when we place God as the star and realize we are only the supporting cast. As a result we are not intimidated, fearful or nasty to others, but we ask "How can I help others, to be even better than I am; how can I encourage them to pursue their passion?" "True confidence and true success is when we help others to succeed."

"There are two kinds of pride, both good and bad 'Good pride' represents our dignity and self-respect.' Bad pride' is the deadly sin of superiority that reeks of conceit and arrogance."

- **John C. Maxwell**

CONCLUSION

"If you set goals and go after them with all the determination you can muster, your gifts will take you places that will amaze you."

\- Les Brown

\-

DETERMINATION TO EMERGE AND GROW

We hope you have enjoyed the journey of gleaning the principles every emerging leader should discover. We hope that as you find your burden your passion, and dream out Loud that God would give you wisdom and strategies to become a world class leader. Whatever fields of leadership you find yourself in remember; your entire objective in life is to make the Master Architect proud.

The accolades of men are encouraging, but we live to receive the ultimate reward and that is our "Well Done from God Himself." Remember that you are a vessel. Decide to be a vessel of Honor. Consecrate yourself from everything that would try to make you a vessel of dishonor. Always keep standards and values as you grow and never allow pride to take over. Keep Pouring into others, after all that's what vessels do they pour. The stage that God has designed for you may not be the same stage He has designed for me or others, but your stage is just as important.

"Life is not Measured by its duration, but its donation"
\-   Dr. Myles Munroe

LEADING A GENERATION

You might be young but you have a gift planted within you. Let determination and compassion be the driving force to propel you forward. Paul encouraged his protégé Timothy:

Let no one despise you for your youth, but set the believers an example in speech, in conduct, in love, in faith, in purity. – 1 Timothy 4:12 ESV

Remember that you must give yourself wholly over to what it is God has called you to do, Cultivate, Meditate, Practice what you were designed to do. Don't do everything and get nowhere, but do the thing (s) you are good at and let your progress be evident to all. "The secret to concentration is elimination"

[13] Until I come, devote yourself to the public reading of Scripture, to exhortation, to teaching. [14] Do not neglect the gift you have, which was given you by prophecy when the council of elders laid their hands on you. [15] Practice these things, immerse yourself in them,[c] so that all may see your progress. [16] Keep a close watch on yourself and on the teaching. Persist in this, for by so doing you will save both yourself and your hearers.
- 1 Timothy 4:13-16 ESV

As Paul prepared to exit the race he was set on by God he made Timothy aware that he remained committed to doing what he was created to do. When you look back over your life, don't let regret haunt you, but let your faithfulness reward you.

"[6] For I am already being poured out as a drink offering, and the time of my departure has come. [7] I have fought the good fight, I have finished the race, I have kept the faith. [8] Henceforth there is laid up for me the crown of righteousness, which the Lord, the righteous judge, will award to me on that Day, and not only to me but also to all who have loved his appearing." – 2 Timothy 4:6-8 ESV

Pour out your best, and Emerge to become a Leader in your generation!

OTHER BOOKS BY THE AUTHORS

Other books Include:

1. The Faith book for Face book:
2. Moments with God for Teens
3. Real Questions Real Answers
4. Reviving a Generation
5. Dreams are not meant to die

For ordering any of the above mentioned books visit any online Book Retailer.

For Booking and engagements email: **madpastor1@gmail.com** or contact 242-336-4207 or 242-439-5504. You can also connect with us on social networks
https://www.facebook.com/duerre.thomas
Or **http://www.facebook.com/sharai.thomas**

Twitter names: madpastord or ladys

We would be grateful if you can please leave a review online at Amazon or the book retailer of your choice for "Leading Generation."

www.ingramcontent.com/pod-product-compliance
Lightning Source LLC
Chambersburg PA
CBHW032216040426
42449CB00005B/630